How to Date a Korean Lady

The English Gentleman's guide
to finding your Seoul mate

Alexander James

Copyright © 2019 Alexander James

All rights reserved.

ISBN-13: 978-1-09-604840-4

CONTENTS

	Foreword	v
	Introduction	1
1	Getting Started	5
2	Making the Connection	11
3	Leading and the Date Course	19
4	How to Behave on a Date	23
5	Wearing Couple Style	31
6	Counting the Days	35
7	Always on Call	41
8	Learning Korean	47
9	Korean Food and Drink	53
10	In the Bedroom	61
11	Meeting her Parents	69
12	Getting Married	75
	Summary	83

FOREWORD

Welcome to this book on "How to date a Korean lady" which has been written by my English gentleman and husband Alexander James. If you have purchased this dating book, then congratulations on making a great choice. This book will be a highly valuable guide to you in successfully dating a Korean lady, as I can personally testify.

I believe that falling in love can help us to discover who we are and to achieve greater self-awareness. Through dating and my relationship with my English gentleman, I discovered that this was indeed true.

As a Korean lady who grew up in Busan and then worked in Seoul for more than 10 years before relocating to Singapore, I always wanted to experience the world beyond Korea. In this respect I felt that I was not a typical Korean lady.

However, through my romantic journey with Alexander from our first date, our engagement and our wedding I discovered that I am most comfortable dating in the Korean style.

I would like to declare that I did not write any part of this book. However, after reading the first draft I realised just how much effort my English gentleman had put into making me comfortable by dating me as a Korean man would have dated me, and this directly contributed to the success of our relationship.

In fact, through reading this book I now understand how different dating culture is in Korea compared to the United Kingdom and I appreciate how much effort Alexander made in learning how to date a Korean lady, in fact much more than I knew when we were dating.

With that I am confident that you will find great value from this book and that the advice contained in the following chapters will greatly increase your probability of success when dating a Korean lady by making her comfortable and happy.

I would like to wish you the best of luck with your international relationship, and always remember that love is the most valuable thing in life, no matter home country or culture.

YS Lee (Mrs Alexander James)

How to Date a Korean Lady

Alexander James

INTRODUCTION

While studying at University in Manchester in the United Kingdom I shared a flat with two overseas students from Hong Kong and this first awakened my passion for Asia. I subsequently joined the Hong Kong and Chinese Society of the University which gave me the opportunity to connect with many of students from the Asia region.

After completing my studies, I moved to London and joined one of the big 5 consulting firms. After being with this firm for almost 10 years and being promoted multiple times to a middle management position I explored the option of transferring to the Hong Kong office. Unfortunately, this did not work out for a couple of reasons and I remained in London.

A couple of years later I left the consulting firm and moved to an enterprise collaboration start-up that was originally founded in San Francisco. I joined as one of the first members of the Europe, Middle East and Africa (EMEA) team based in London.

After this start-up was acquired by one of largest IT companies in the world, I jumped at the opportunity to relocated to Singapore in 2013 to lead an Asia wide team. Through living in Singapore and travelling throughout Asia with work and on vacation I met and made friends with Asian ladies from many countries including Singapore, Malaysia, China, Hong Kong, Japan and of course South Korea.

Around 6 months after moving to Singapore I met an amazing Korean lady in a business meeting. Her beautiful smile, bright pink lipstick and amazing happy energy made a huge first impression on me. From that initial meeting I knew that I wanted to become friends with this lady and get to know her better. However, at no time did I think that a couple of years later that she would become my wife. In fact, she was so amazing that I thought that she might not even talk to me outside the meeting. I guess that it shows if you are brave and a gentleman, that great things can happen to you.

This book captures the lessons that I learnt from dating and marrying a Korean lady, both my success and failures. I am also friends with several other Korean ladies who are in international relationships with non-Korean men. Therefore, I have included their insights in this book to provide a broader perspective on best practices and what any gentleman attempting of dating a Korean lady should know.

Additionally, I also read over 50 blog posts and watched many YouTube videos to help me learn how to date a Korean lady during the early stages of my relationship. So, I will also include these insights in this book and share links to some of the most insightful ones in the relevant chapters. I have tried to write the book that I would have wanted to read when I started dating a Korean lady, but that did not exist at the time.

This book is intended to help you find and build a long-term successful relationship with a Korean lady. All ladies, Korean or otherwise are special and unique, therefore my advice may not apply to every Korean lady, but it will certainly be relevant to many of them.

The key thing that you should take away from this book is that if you try to date a Korean lady as you would date a western lady you will probably fail. You need to date a Korean lady as a Korean man would date her to be successful.

Alexander James

CHAPTER 1:
GETTING STARTED

So why would you want to date a Korean lady and what makes Korean ladies so special?

Korean ladies are highly educated, intelligent, strong, independent and ambitious. They have attractive personalities, are adventurous, cosmopolitan and curious about the world. Compared to other Asian countries many Korean ladies will have studies overseas, giving them a more international outlook. Often you will see a group of Korean ladies exploring the world together, but I have never seen a group of Korean men doing the same thing.

Korean ladies are recognised worldwide as being the most attractive in Asia. They are generally taller than other Asians ladies, they are beautiful, have the best skin, have great figures, dress fashionably and always have perfect hair and makeup. They are feminine, cute, lovely, sexy, funny, attentive, thoughtful and have a strong desire to make their partner happy. Of all the ladies in Asia, Korean ladies are the most highly desirable, and they know this. Korea ladies are absolutely "Not" easy.

From the paragraphs above you will understand that Korean ladies are amazing and should be highly prized as your partner. However, Korean ladies are aware of how attractive and desirable they are. Therefore, they have high standards for any gentleman that wants to date them.

Firstly, a Korean lady will expect you to be well educated and to be successful in your chosen career. Many Korean ladies are more than capable of earning their own money; however, they will expect you to show that you can care and provide for them. Despite progress in recent years Korean ladies do not equality with Korean men when it comes to careers, money and family responsibilities.

Korean ladies take on certain obligations be becoming a wife to a Korean man, not only to her husband but also to his parents and family. For example, she will be expected to prepare food to be served at traditional ceremonies for her husband's family throughout the year.

Being a man is Korea also come with its own set of challenges, particularly financial ones. A Korean man is expected to provide for his wife and his family. A Korean man with a low paid job or without a job will not be able to marry, and if he cannot marry then he will not be able to have a family of his own.

Korean ladies like successful, mature, responsible and ambitious men who have value, purpose, dream, aspirations and goals that they are striving to achieve. For example, when meeting for the first time some ladies may ask what you do and which company you work for before asking your name. Korean ladies have many men who would like to date them, so how are you going to stand out?

It is also important that you demonstrate that you can provide for her financially and will be able to care for her in the future. Korean ladies like their partners to have well paid jobs, to drive a nice car, to take them to nice restaurants and to buy them nice gifts. On a date with a Koran lady the man is usually expected to pay for everything. Focus on ensuring that the Korean lady feels that she does not have to worry about money and can focus on being lovely and romantic. We will cover more on this topic in Chapter 4: How to Behave on a Date.

Korean men are required to serve 2 years of compulsory military service. Korean ladies expect the man to be at least as successful as them and earning at least as much as them. Therefore, dating a man who is 2-4 years older than them is the norm and even desirable for many Korean ladies. Increasing numbers of Korean men, especially those who live outside of major cities are finding it harder to find Korean wives as their exceptions are increasing. This is leading to these Korean men marrying increasing numbers ladies from China and other South East Asian countries.

A Korean lady is always impeccably dressed with perfect hair and makeup. Therefore, she is not going to date you if you do not make an effort with your appearance. So, go to the gym to build a good physique (slim is generally more prized than muscular) and dress stylishly.

You can learn a lot from Korean men when it comes to fashion and male grooming. On the topic of male grooming I have via my wife discovered an appreciation for Korean face masks. My favourite brand being the Mediheal Aquaring Mask. Using one of these masks for 20 minutes after shaving makes my skin incredible smooth and look 10 years younger.

As a non-Korea you will have some advantages when it comes to dating a Korean lady. For example, you will be taller than most Korean men and there is an appreciation for Caucasian features including a small face and high nose. There is also an expectation that you will treat her more as an equal than a Korean man might, and she may be able to escape the daughter-in-law obligations that she would encounter when marring a Korean man.

In summary, Korean ladies are the most desirable in Asia, but at the same time they have high expectations for any man, Korean or otherwise who wants to date them. Therefore, you should focus on being a successful man in your chosen profession and presenting yourself well before trying to date a Korean lady.

If you want to successfully date a Korean lady, you will need to do it the Korean way. This includes Clothes, Food, Language, Dating Etiquette etc. and this is what we will cover in the following chapters.

How to Date a Korean Lady

Alexander James

CHAPTER 2:
MAKING THE CONNECTION

In the UK it would not be unusual to approach a lady on the street or in a cafe. However, making the initial connection is South Korea is rather different.

Firstly, Korean ladies are not supposed to talk to strangers, in fact it would be considered weird to do so. Talking to a stranger means that you have no friends or family to talk to, which would be embarrassing and even shameful. Even if you were to approach a Korean lady on the street or in a cafe, she may not speak enough English to understand you or be confident enough to reply to you.

One of my female Korean friends explained that it is not normal for a Korean lady to send time one on one with a man that she is not dating, and many Korean ladies would be uncomfortable doing so. Therefore, proceed with caution and tread gently if you do try approaching a Korean lady.

It is also important to appreciate than some Korean ladies will open or even prefer to date a non-Korean man, others will date only Korean men.

Traditionally, many Korean couples meet through mutual friends or informal dating events for groups of friends rather than as individuals. I guess there is safety in numbers and that this reduced the risk of someone being a total stranger as there is some existing connection, at least at a peer group level.

Blind dates may be rather unusual or even antiquated in the UK today, but they are still very common in Korea as a popular way to meet a potential partner, and come in several varieties:
- **So-gae-ting:** A blind date for just the couple (소개팅)
- **Mi-ting:** A blind date where a group of ladies meet a group of men (미팅)
- **Mat-seon:** A blind date that is organized by the couple's parents (맞선)

In some instances, families may introduce potential partners if they get desperate as the lady or man gets older without being married, or at least in a serious relationship with the potential to get married in the future. One of my friends mentioned that her parents arranged an introduction for her to one of their friend's son's. After a lot of pressure, she finally agreed to go on the date. However, she behaved so badly towards the man on the date that her parents did not try to match make for her ever again.

Make some Korean friends and they will invite you to social group gatherings where you can meet Korean ladies. By having Korean friends, you will also appear safer than a stranger as you will already have an appreciation and respect for Korean culture.

If you don't have a group of Korean friends who can invite you to social gatherings with groups of ladies, then online dating can be a great option. As with many other countries online dating and mobile dating apps are growing in popularity in South Korea. Popular ones include HelloTalk, 1km, Badoo, Bumble, Tinder, KoreanCupid, Azar, Noondate, MEEFF, OkCupid and Skout. Online dating is a safe way for Korean ladies interested to meet foreigners and are increasing in popularity for this reason. Meeting online also provides the Korean lady a way to hide her western partner from her traditional and conservative parents.

Some mobile apps also include built in language translation from Korean to English and other languages which might be helpful if you do not speak Korean. However, many South Korean ladies that you will meet online can already speak good English.

However, if you are in Seoul and feeling brave then there are a few areas where you can try to meet Korean ladies, on the street, in bars or in clubs. In Itaewon, Hongdae and Gangnam you may find Korean ladies who speak some English and who are interested to meet and date foreigners.

Hongdae is a popular university area with lots of young ladies in their early 20s, it is also home to the largest lesbian night club in Korea. This is one area in Seoul where Koran ladies will be more adventurous in their appearance, you will see brightly coloured hair, unconventional fashions and even tattoos which are generally taboo in Korea. Hongdae has numerous bars and clubs that cater to young ladies curious about foreigners, therefore it a good place to meet adventurous Korea ladies who speak good English.

Itaewon is more upscale than Hongdae and as a result more popular for professional ladies in the mid to late 20s and early 30s. It is particularly famous for its night life and delicious Korean BBQ restaurants. Itaweon is a popular and well-known foreigner area in Seoul, so you will find ladies here who are open to an international relationship.

The most expensive area to meet ladies in Seoul is Gangnam, yes, the one made globally famous in 2012 by the song "Gangnam Style". This is going to be the most challenging location to meet Korean ladies as they will be the most demanding for image, status and money. As a result, you will find fewer foreigners in Gangnam at night compared to either Hongdae or Itaweon, so you will stand out more. However, Gangnam will have the largest number of the most beautiful women so you might want to explore and try out the trendy high-end night clubs here.

South Korea is very homogeneous as the population is over 99% Korean. Therefore, even today it is relatively rare to see international couples even in Seoul. For example, my wife and I have walked around central Seoul together for a whole day and sometimes not seen one other international couple.

Be prepared, if you are dating a Korean lady you will stand out, you may get stared at on a regular basis by complete strangers. People in Korea generally try to fit in and conform. Therefore, any Korean lady dating a foreigner is taking a risk by dating you.

Many Korean ladies have heard stories of the English language teachers coming to Korea for six to twelve months, dating Korean ladies and then returning to their home country at the end of the contact leaving her behind and heart broken. Therefore, they will naturally be cautious when considering a relationship with a non-Korean man. As a result, you must always behave as a gentleman to protect her reputation. We will discuss this topic in more detail in Chapter 4: How to Behave on a Date.

You also need to be aware that Korean men may object to you dating a Korean lady, as they may think that you are stealing one of their women. In practice Korean ladies are intelligent, mature and will make their own decisions about the men they want to have relationships with. However, Korean men may even try to put pressure on the lady or shame her into not dating with you, or even physically try to pull her away from you.

The more attractive the lady, the more strongly Korean men will object to you dating her. The reason for this behaviour is that Korean men are both insecure and jealous of the advantages that you have as a non-Korean man. Korean society places expectations and obligations on the Korean man just as it does the Korean lady. As a foreigner you are free from these constraints. Hopefully, you will not experience this territorial behaviour personally, but at least you will now be prepared if you do.

Younger Korean ladies may date men for fun that they would never consider marrying, which may include you as a non-Korean man. However, as that lady enters her mid-twenties, she will start to think seriously about marriage rather than simply dating for fun. There is a saying in Korea that ladies are like Christmas. It is best on the 25th, great on the 26th, still OK on the 31st, but less desirable after that.

However, the age at which couples marry in Korean is increasing. For example, in 2009 the average age of first marriage is 31.6 years for men and 28.7 years for women according to Korea National Statistical Office. In 2017 the average age of first marriage had increased to 32.9 years for men and 30.2 years for women. As we discussed in the opening chapter it is normal for men to date ladies 2-4 years younger than themselves, and this trend appears to be consistent even as the age of the first marriage is increasing.

In the UK couples tend to start out as friends going for coffee or drink after work. Gradually this moves to watching a movie or having dinner. Then at some point they become a couple. There does not tend to be a conversation where you agree you are now in a relationship; it just sort of happens.

However, in Korea you need to let the lady know that you are interested in her as more than a friend, or she will not know. Be clear in your intentions. If you want a to have a "friends with benefits" type relation let her know. If you want a long-term relationship that could lead to marriage in in the future let her know. This may feel rather strange and unromantic, but it will help to avoid any misunderstandings and is very normal in Korea.

My wife and I had been friends for a couple of years when she sat be down and explained the reasons why she thought I would make a good partner and even future husband for her. She was very clear and intentional that she wanted a relationship with me, not just to go on a date. Talking about marriage before the first date would be very unusual in the UK and would have scared many men off. However, I appreciated her being intentional in setting out her expectations with me, and this is intentional communication is something that has continued throughout our relationship.

As you will discover in Chapter 6: Counting the Days if you do have an official day 1 of your relationship you will not know how long you have been dating and as a result you will not know when to celebrate the key milestones in your relationship. But, more to come on that important topic later.

In summary, couples in Korea typically meet via mutual friends rather than making an approach on the street or in a cafe. Additionally, online and mobile dating is growing and can help you as a non-Korean. When it comes to progressing the relationship always be clear and explain your intentions, if you don't tell the lady that you want to be more than friends she will not know.

Alexander James

CHAPTER 3:
LEADING AND THE DATE COURSE

So, you have found that special Korean lady, you have clearly communicated your intentions and she has agreed to go on a date with you.

When dating in the UK you would typically ask the lady where she would like to go on a date. However, Korean ladies expect the man to have planned out the whole date in advance. If a man tried to tell his date in the UK what they were doing and where they were going on a date without consulting her, then he is very unlikely to get a second date, or even a first date.

I did not fully understand the concept of "leading" until probably our second month of dating. We had been to the cinema together, I had picked the movie and booked/paid for the seats, so a good start in leading the date. However, as we came out of the cinema, I asked by date what she would like to do next. This question was greeted with a look that combined disappointment and confusion. After a few minutes of awkwardly looking at each other, I suggested that we went for a coffee and the date continued.

This was a tipping point for me as a realised that the consultative dating approach that I was familiar with from the UK was not working with my Korean lady and that I needed to revise my dating approach. I did some research and spoke with other Korean ladies and they explained to me the concept of leading and the date course.

To date a Korean lady, you should be prepared and have the whole date (aka the Date Course) planned out from beginning to end, for example:

- We will meet at the cinema at 2:30pm for the 3pm showing (pick the movie and book the tickets in advance)
- After the movie we will go for coffee at this café and shopping at this mall (make sure both are close by and easily accessible)
- In the evening we will have dinner at this restaurant (book a table) followed by drinks at this bar (make a reservation)

I modified my approach to dating and future dates went much more smoothly. But why to Korean ladies like the man to lead the date?

This is partly because this demonstrates that you have thought about the date and made an effort to make the date enjoyable for her. But there is another even more important reason that you may not be aware of. Professional working women they typically need to interact with male colleagues, customers and partners every day. They need to be organised, logical, analytical and structured, taking on a more masculine persona and mindset.

Through the man leading the date the lady can relax knowing that she is being cared for, enabling her to reconnect with her feminine side and become lovelier. Therefore, by leading the date you will help your Korean lady become more open to romance. This is very much a return to the more traditional male and female gender relationship roles.

Now this expectation to lead the date can feel a bit pressured or stressful for someone who is not used to this Korean style of dating. Therefore, to minimise any potential stress it helps to be prepared. For example, I keep a list of date ideas, restaurants, cafes and bars on my phone that I regularly add to, like my own personal date course reference guide. I now enjoy leading our dates, it has helped me to embrace my masculine side while also helping my wife to embrace her feminine side.

Finally, it is important to let your Korean lady know what outfit and especially what shoes will be suitable for the date course. If your date turns up wearing her best Jimmy Choo shoes and you take her hiking in the countryside, she will be less than impressed.

In summary, the Korean lady will expect the man to lead the date. By planning an end to end date course, the gentleman can help the lady to reconnect with her feminine side and to become more open to romance. Being organised can help to manage any pressure that may come from the expectation on the gentleman to lead the date.

Alexander James

CHAPTER 4:
HOW TO BEHAVE ON A DATE

As a western man in Korea you can be easily stereotyped as a playboy by Korean ladies. Similarly, Korean ladies are very protective of their reputation and do not want to appear easy. As we discussed in the previous chapter, Korean ladies will be more cautious about dating with you than dating with a Korean man.

Therefore, you need to show that you are a gentleman and not a playboy to build her trust and demonstrate that you are looking for a meaningful long-term relationship. Take things slowly and don't try to escalate the relationship to something intimate too soon or you will only prove the playboy stereotype to be correct.

When on a date with a Korean lady always treat her with respect and kindness, try to make her feel special all the time. She is an intelligent, sophisticated and independent lady, but she will still enjoy being treated like a princess. For example, open the door for her when entering and leaving buildings or getting into or out of a car. Pull a chair out for her and then push it forwards as she stars to sit down. Hold her hand when she is walking up or down stairs, especially if she is wearing high heels.

Lots of Korean ladies like to wear very short shorts and very short skirts so you should always be ready to protect her modesty. When she is getting out of a car, getting off a high bar stool etc, stand in front of her so that no one catches a sight of something that they should not. One thing that my wife likes, and which was recommended by her mother was for me to stand behind her when she is going up an escalator to prevent any up skirting. And similarly standing in front of her on the way down and escalator for the same reason.

When going on a date a Korean lady will make a huge effort to look her best for you. Hair, makeup, outfit, shoes, handbag and accessories will all be perfect. However, as a result she will often be late arriving for your date. Therefore, always allow some contingency for this in your date course planning, a 30-minute buffer should be. When she arrives tell her how beautiful she looks and how amazing her Outfit Of The Day (OOTD) is. Absolutely, do not complain about the fact that she is late and has kept you waiting.

If your Korean lady asks you to buy her something, then as long as you can afford it then I would highly recommend doing so. For example, my wife found a beautiful pair of Jimmy Choo shoes in the sale that she loved. She could afford to buy them for herself but asked me to buy them for her as a birthday gift, as she would love them even more if they came from me.

It is also completely normal for boyfriends and husbands to carry a Korean lady's handbag. Initially this feels very strange and embarrassing for an English gentleman, especially if it is bright pink and fluffy. But now it is completely normal to carry my wife's handbag. I don't do it all the time, but when I do, she really likes it and finds it very romantic.

Be prepared that your Korean lady may act very cute and even childish on your date. This is called Aegyo (애교) which roughly translates as baby-like behaviors. She may speak to you in a different voice than she does to her friends and may make many cute physical gestures towards you. As with carrying her handbag, this may feel a little unconformable initially, but she is showing you and everyone else how much she likes you and how much she is enjoying being with you on a date. Therefore, my advice is to embrace this cute behaviour and enjoy the experience.

However, beware that some Korean ladies may use this powerful technique as a secret weapon to get what they want from their partner. For example, taking her to a specific restaurant, driving across the city to pick her up or buying her a new designer handbag.

You may be surprised that some ladies in their twenties and even early thirties who live at home with their parents still have a curfew. This would be very rare in the UK; however, it is much more common than you might think in Korea. Therefore, if your date tells you that she has a 10pm curfew you should respect this rather than making fun of her.

Make sure that your date is always home before her curfew. As you will discover in Chapter 11: Meeting her Parents you want to make the best possible impression on her parents and show that you are respectable when you are finally introduced to them. You should escort your lady back to her home at the end of the date, even if it is on the other side of town to ensure that she gets home safely. If this is not possible, at the very least make that you help her to catch a taxi home and offer to pay the fare.

Generally, a Korean lady will expect the man to pay for everything during the date including food, coffee, drinks, entry tickets, taxi etc. It is not that the Korean ladies are very materialistic as per the way many mainland Chinese ladies are stereotyped. It is rather that they want to be confident that the man can take care of them and is willing to do so.

If you pay for dinner, then the lady may offer to pay for desert or coffee later. If she does offer, then you should allow her to pay. Otherwise, assume that you will pay for everything on your dates. Think back to the point about dating for marriage rather than fun that we mentioned in Chapter 2: Making the Connection. This is another reason why many Korean ladies are looking for men who are slightly older, who are already successful and established in their career can who can support her financially.

As the man is responsible to pay for the majority of the dates this can make dating an expensive activity for the man. Therefore, many Korean men will take advantage of offers, vouchers, loyalty schemes and special promotions at restaurants and attractions to save some money. This is completely expected, and Korean ladies are unlikely to look down on you for being cheap for doing so. Therefore, you should not feel embarrassed about taking advantage of these opportunities to save some money to put towards your next date.

Let me share a mistake that I personally made on our first official date. After a fun but slightly nervous date to the Singapore Aquarium we went to a nearby restaurant for dinner (which I had not booked or researched). When it came time to pay the bill, I suggested that we split the bill 50/50 which would be very normal in the UK. This was met with a rather surprised look from my date, but we both handed over our credit cards and the restaurant bill was split evenly.

The next week my wife explained that Korean couples don't go Dutch and split the bill. She explained that in Korea friends split the bill, but couples do not. Rather the man pays for everything as I explained earlier, or they take it in turns to pay if they want to share the costs.

Korean ladies are more becoming successful in their own careers, more affluent and are looking for greater equality in society. Therefore, you may find that some Korean ladies are open or even keen to share the dating costs. My date was of this mind set and said that she would prefer to take turns to pay rather than splitting the bill. In the end I think that I ended up paying for 70-80% of our dates, and I did not ever suggest that we split the bill again.

While we are discussing money, this is a good time to share how Korean couples manage their finances once they get married.

In the UK, a couple who are both employed would typically have their salary paid into their personal accounts. Then each month they will transfer an agreed amount into a joint account that is used to cover living expenses e.g. rent/mortgage, food, travel, petrol, utility bills, council tax. Of course, there are other models, but this is typical for the majority of professional couples that I know in the UK.

However, in Korea things are rather different. Typically, a Korean husband will have all his monthly salary into an account managed by his wife. Certainly, this is the case for both of my Korean sisters-in-law. From his salary the wife will manage the living costs for the family and will also give the husband a small allowance that he can spend on whatever he likes each month. Interestingly it is not possible for couple to open a joint account in Korea even if they wanted to.

Hallie Bradley has two great blog posts on her website The Soul of Seoul which you can read if you are interested in understanding more about managing money after marriage in Korea:
- ➢ How Much Allowance Do You Get?
- ➢ Can We Open a Joint Account?

In summary, always be a gentleman on a date including taking steps protect your lady's reputation and modesty. Plan that your date will probably be late and respect that she may have a curfew that she needs to keep. Be prepared to pay for everything on your date and do not suggest splitting the bill.

How to Date a Korean Lady

Alexander James

CHAPTER 5:
WEARING COUPLE STYLE

Korea as a society has a more conservative culture compared to the UK, Europe and the US. Therefore, Public Displays of Affection (PDA) like kissing and hugging are much less common than you may be used to, and may even be founded upon by some Koreans, especially from the older generation.

This is linked to my earlier recommendation about always protecting the lady's reputation. If a lady is seen displaying affection in public, she may be criticised, potentially even more so with a non-Korean.

Society is changing, and of course Korean couples hold hands, hug and kiss in public. However, it is important to recognise that not every Korean lady will be comfortable with this. Therefore, go easy on the PDA, talk to her about what she is comfortable with and respect her preferences.

This is where Korean couple style comes in with couples dressing alike to show that they are in a relationship. This can be as subtle as just wearing a matching pair of shoes or baseball caps, or as obvious as head to toe matching outfits including accessories. And it's not just the outside clothes that other people can see. My wife's sisters gave my wife and I matching Calvin Klein underwear as a first Christmas gift.

Some couples also wear matching couple rings. These are not engagement rings, but they do signify that the couple are in a committed relationship. Couple rings are typically exchanged around 100 days into the relationship.

At first, I was not keen on wearing couple style with my wife, recalling the terrible couple outfits from my parents' generation. However, having experienced couple style myself it can actually be cute and fun. My wife and I have several matching outfits including matching swimwear that we wore on our honeymoon, that we have fun wearing together on dates from time to time.

You should also recognise that most Korean ladies have an inner "Shopping Goddess" and that many Korean ladies would even quote shopping as their main hobby. Shopping is certainly a very popular date activity, at least for the lady. If your date wants to go shopping be patient, carry her bags and be engaged in the shopping process.

Do not complain about how long it is taking, how much money she is spending, why she does not need another pair of expensive shoes. Worship her shopping goddess regularly and she will be very happy and grateful. Also, you might want to ask your Korean lady to pick out clothes for you that she would like you to wear so that you look good when on dates with her.

In summary, my recommendation is to be prepared that your Korean lady may suggest you try couple style. If she does then go for it, you may feel a bit self-conscious, but you will probably enjoy it. Remember, that by wearing couple style she wants everyone to know that you are her partner and she is proud to be seen with you.

Alexander James

CHAPTER 6:
COUNTING THE DAYS

In the UK couples would typically celebrate their anniversary once per year, valentine's day on the 14th February and Christmas Day with an exchange of cards, gifts and a romantic dinner. However, in Korea there are many more days that a couple can choose to celebrate.

As we touched on briefly in Chapter 2: Making the Connection it is important to know the first day of your relationship so that you can count how many days that you have been dating, as you will discover in this chapter.

100 Days

Rather than months or years Korean couples measure relationships in multiples of 100 days. The first 100 day celebration being the most import. In fact, some couples only celebrate their 100 day anniversary.

With my wife we celebrated every 100 day anniversary up to and including 1,000 days. Some celebrations were larger and more lavish, others were smaller and more intimate. This was often due to how the day aligned with other celebrations (see below) and our travel schedule with work. But we celebrated every one of them together, and this is what is most important.

As with leading the date the onus is very much on the man to plan these celebrations. For the first 100 day celebration with my wife I arranged a nice lunch at a great cafe that we both liked and brought her a romantic gift. After lunch at the cafe I gave my wife a card that I had personally designed and had printed. She was very happy to receive as she had no idea that I knew anything about the Korea 100 day tradition.

After lunch we went back to my apartment where I presented her with the gift that I had arranged for her. This was a luxury leather handbag by an English designer that I had purchased a month earlier on a business trip to the UK. I'm not advising that you crazy and spend more than you can afford, but I am advising that you do make your first 100 day celebration special for your special Korean lady.

The 14th of every month

We are probably all familiar with Valentine's Day which is celebrated on 14th February each year. A typical Valentine's Day celebration involves exchanging cards and gifts followed by a romantic dinner. Often the man will also buy the lady flowers on Valentine's Day, with red roses being the most popular and widely available option.

However, in Korea couples celebrate on the 14th of almost every month and there are effectively two Valentines days. On February 14th ladies give cards and gifts to the man. One month later on the 14th March which is called White Day, the man gives cards and gifts to the lady. Not all couples celebrate every event every month, but here is the full list:

- **Valentine's Day (Feb 14th):** Valentine's day in Korea is a day that lady gives gifts to the man
- **White Day (March 14th):** This is the day for the men to give gifts to the lady (second Valentine's day)
- **Black day (April 14th):** This is a day when single people meet up to drown their sorrows by eating a bowl of black noodles. Not really a couple celebration day, but interesting to know about and is included here for completeness
- **Rose Day (May 14th):** Couples exchange roses
- **Kiss Day (June 14th):** People kiss everyone they meet (very conservatively)
- **Silver Day (July 14th):** Couples exchange silver gifts and accessories
- **Green Day (August 14th):** Couples enjoy a natural place, whilst drinking soju (Korean alcohol) which comes in a green bottle
- **Photo Day (September 14th):** Couples take a photo together and put it somewhere nice to look at
- **Wine Day (October 14th):** Couples enjoy a glass of wine together
- **Movie Day (November 14th):** Couples watch a movie together
- **Hug Day (December 14th):** People hug each other to keep warm in the winter

Other Special Days

There are also a number of additional days on which a Korean couple may choose to celebrate their relationship:

- **Diary Day (January 1st):** Couples share diaries to celebrate the year to come. Which given the number of celebration days to keep track of is probably a very practical gift.
- **Pepero Day (11th November):** Pepero is a brand

of popular snack in Korea. It has long thin round biscuit dipped in different typically chocolate based coatings. If you write 11th November as 11/11 it resembles the Pepero sticks. On this day couples give boxes of Pepero to their partners. Manufactures also produce special flavours and packaging to boost sales on this day. Pepero is manufactured by Lotte which is one of the largest conglomerates in Korea and the tag line is "Pepero – Love at First Stick" which is rather appropriate.

- **Christmas Eve (December 24th):** In the UK my family have always celebrated and exchanged gifts on Christmas day. However, Korean couples like to celebrate by going out for a date and having a drink on Christmas Eve. I'm not quite sure how but I completely missed this important point in my dating research, and my wife had not communicated to me that this was something that she wanted us to do. Therefore, if you want to avoid my mistake and having a disappointed lady on Christmas Eve remember to take her out for a date or at least arrange a romantic drink at home.

Birthdays

In Korea some people celebrate their birthday based on the Lunar calendar rather than Gregorian Calendar. Therefore, their birthday on the Gregorian Calendar will be on a different day each year. To give you an example if your lady was born on 4th day of the 8th month of the Lunar calendar her birthday according to the Gregorian Calendar would be as follows:

- **2015:** 16th September
- **2016:** 4th September
- **2017:** 23rd September
- **2018:** 13th September

- **2019:** 2nd September
- **2020:** 20th September

In summary, you need to be very organised to date a Korean lady and there are many celebrations to plan for, even if you do not celebrate every one of these dates together every year. The 100 day celebration is the most important and there are two Valentines Days in Korea.

Alexander James

CHAPTER 7:
ALWAYS ON CALL

With many high-tech devices companies like Samsung and LG being founded in South Korea, combined with high speed 4G networks and the huge popularity of online gaming like PlayerUnknown's Battlegrounds (PUBG) and of course Star Craft, it should come as no surprise that the mobile phone plays a key role in dating a Korean lady.

As we touched on in Chapter 4: How to Behave on a Date by merit of being a non-Korean man you will be stereotyped as a playboy. Therefore, in the early stages of your relationship with a Korean lady she may ask to see your phone and check your chat history so that she can confirm that you can be trusted and that you are not seeing any other ladies. If she asks, then hand over your phone without hesitation as this will build trust. Any resistance and complaining about your privacy will only confirm that you are a playboy who cannot be trusted.

Social media has become part of everyone's life over the last couple of years, but possibly even more so in Korea. It is important to recognize that Korean ladies are in an online competition to show that they the happiest, that they are in the best relationship and that they have the best partner. She will also be following her friends updates on social media and comparing their relationships to her own. The restaurants that you take her to, the dates that you take her on and the gifts that you buy her will all be photographed, posted online and critiqued by her friends.

This competitiveness and the high beauty standards have made South Korea the plastic surgery capital of the world. On one business trip to Seoul I had my own Crazy Rich Asians experience. Two ladies carrying an excessive number of designer shopping bags that they stuffed into the overhead bins were seated next to me. One was taking pain killers and anti-inflammatory drugs during the flight. The incisions behind her ears from her recent facelift were clearly evident, as was the yellow staining from the iodine solution used to disinfect the area before surgery. The second lady was wearing huge sunglasses for the whole flight in an attempt to disguise her recent double eyelid surgery.

It is vital to keep your mobile phone with you at all times and to never miss a call from your Korean lady. If you do not answer she may start to worry that she is not a priority to you or that you are with another lady and that is why you did not respond. You should also be proactive and call her every day, a call in the evening before bed is the minimum that will be expected.

The most popular messaging app in Korean is KakaoTalk. You can think of KakaoTalk as being the Korean version of WeChat, Line and WhatsApp. But the unique thing about KakaoTalk is the huge number emojis available. There are literally thousands of sets of emojis that you can download for free or purchase. Sometimes you will see a KakaoTalk conversation composed entirely of emoji without any text.

Therefore, if you have not done so already download the KakaoTalk app from the relevant app store for your mobile phone and start getting familiar with the features and of course those emoji. Next keep your phone with you at all times and always be ready to respond to a message from your lady. As with calls, if you take too long to reply the lady may feel that she is not a priority to you, and that is going to make getting another date much more challenging. Be proactive and send the lady a cute message without waiting for her to initiate every conversation.

Korean ladies are very social media savvy and are keen to take a selfie showing off their Outfit Of The Day (OOTD). So always be ready to take a photo of her if she asks, no matter if you are embarrassed or feel self-conscious doing so in a busy public space. Spend some time researching how to take better photos on your mobile phone via online articles or buy a book. Even just taking the time to understand the different modes on your phone e.g. Portrait mode on the iPhone X or thinking about composition, the rule of thirds and lighting can make a huge difference.

Korean ladies perceive that Westerners have a small face which they find attractive. By comparison, some Korean ladies may feel that their face looks larger and therefore less feminine or attractive. Therefore, you can try moving slightly closer to the camera that your lady to even out your face sizes in the photo. You always want to capture your lady looking her best.

I normally take a 4-5 photos from 2-3 different angles each time and let my wife pick the best ones from the 8-15 photos that I have taken. Additionally, always be ready to take a photo with your lady if she asks you to. Don't be shy or hesitate to jump right in. She is proud of you and wants to take a photo with you to share with her friends. Consider buying a selfie stick to give help you improve the creativity and quality of your couple photographs.

In addition to the built-in photo apps there are many photo and beauty apps in Korea. These can be used to improve the quality of the photo e.g. applying soft focus or to retouch the photo for example smoothing out skin tones to give a flawless complexion. Snow and B612 are currently the most popular apps. B612 is targeted at a younger audience, so it likely that your lady will be using Snow rather than B612. Snow also includes facial recognition capabilities and can overlay cute cartoon sticker features e.g. Rabbit nose and ears over the face of each person in the photo.

There are also special couple apps in Korea designed to enhance the communication between couples and keep conversations private. Probably the best known is "Between" that is now also available outside of Korea. The creator of Between stated that his app is so popular in South Korea that he estimates that one in five couples uses it regularly. There are other couple apps that you may want to investigate some of these apps can include 100 day count down timers and reminders of other special celebration days that can come in handy for the less organised man.

In summary, mobile messaging is a key communication channel for couples, so install KakaoTalk today. Proactively send messages to your Korean lady using lots of emoji and remember to respond to messages from your lady promptly. Always be ready to take a photo of your lady or appear in a photo with her, and invest some time learning how to take better photos.

How to Date a Korean Lady

Alexander James

CHAPTER 8:
LEARNING KOREAN

If you cannot speak any Korean initially you will be relying on the lady's English ability to make your relationship possible, as was the case when I first met my wife. However, you should not assume that all Koreans speak English. It may be taught in school but only a small proportion of Korean people will be confident and capable of having and English conversion, yet alone building a long-term relationship conducted in English.

Interestingly, for my wife and I we found that having different first languages was actually a strength for us. We agreed at the outset of our relationship to always be clear in our communications and not to assume that the other would or could assume some meaning or context from something that we alluded to, or which may have been implied based on a shared cultural background, that we did not have. Similarly, we agreed that if we did not understand something that we would keep asking for clarification until we did understand.

Learning some Korean is going to be very important especially when meeting her family, but we will cover than in a later chapter. It will also make you feel more comfortable when visiting Korea and it will make the experience that much more enjoyable.

There are several options for learning Korean. You could take Korean language classes, buy a book or purchase an online course. An American colleague who moved to Japan and who is now married to a Japanese lady went to translator school every night after work for several years to learn Japanese. This was a very intensive experience where he was required to learn 10 new words/phrases every single evening. He is now fluent in Japanese, but this deep dive approach is not for everyone.

For me learning foreign languages has always been challenging, even back at school in the UK where I learnt French, this was never my favourite subject or my best subject for that matter. However, this time around I had great motivation to learn a new language.

I learnt Korean from my wife who became my teacher. I was also lucky to have two other Korean ladies working on the same floor as me in the office who were friends with my wife, and they became my unofficial Korean tutors. Each time we meet in the office we would spend 5 minutes practicing the words or phrases that I was currently learning. They also helped to suggest and teach me new romantic words that I could say to surprise my wife, more of those to follow shortly.

This is not a book on how to learn Korean, rather this chapter will provide a light introduction to Korean and share a couple of useful words and phrases that you can use to express your emotions to a Korean Lady.

I also found that there are many great channels on YouTube for learning Korean. The first one that I found and one this still my favourite is Prof Oh with her "Sweet & Tasty TV" channel featuring KWOW (Korean Word of the Week).

The first Korean word that my wife taught me was "Jin Jja" (진짜) which means "Really". This is a simple and commonly used work that can be used as both as a statement and as a question. In learning Korean, I took a very practical approach. Rather than starting with learning the basics of the alphabet and grammar as you would in an academic course, I focused on learning to say words that I would use regularly.

We used an online notebook that is shared between us on our mobile phones to add in the words that I am trying to learn. Initially romantic words and compliments made up 50% of my vocabulary, as my wife taught me the words that she wants to hear.

My wife even added audio recordings of her saying the words for me so that I can practice when she was not around. We use Microsoft OneNote that comes with all O365 subscriptions, but you could have used Evernote or any of the other similar note taking apps that are available.

For each Korean word we worked out a phonetic way to write the word using Latin characters that made sense to me and which I could replicate. These were rather different to the phonetic pronunciations that I have in academic textbooks. But it worked for me and that was what was important.

I also quickly learned that the grammar is quite simple, but also the opposite of English. A good rule to know is that you always put the subject, the thing that you are talking about first. If you think how Yoda from Star Wars speaks you will get the general idea. For example, in English you would say to a taxi driver "Take me to the Hotel." Where as in Korean this would be "Hotel there take me." In Korean this would be "Hotel Ga Joo Se Yo" (Hotel 가 주세요).

I had the benefit of frequently travelling to Korean for work and this gave me the opportunity to practice my Korean with colleagues, customers and in shops and restaurants. My first big success was walking into the cafe beneath my office in Seoul and ordering my lunch in Korean.

The server responded by asking me, in Korean, if I wanted to eat in or take away. At this point I have not learnt those words (I have now). But the fact that the server thought I would be able to understand and respond to his question in Korean was the first big success for me.

Here are some useful phrases and romantic words that you might want to learn to impress your Korean lady with my phonetic pronunciation notes:

- **Hello:** An Nyoung Ha See Yo (안녕하세요)
- **Nice to meet you:** Ban Ga Wah Yo (반가워요)
- **Goodbye:** An Nyoung He Geh Seh Yo (안녕히 계세요)
- **Thank You:** Gaam Sa Ham Knee Da (감사합니다)
- **Awesome:** Day Dan Hae Yo (대단해요)
- **Goddess:** Yu Shin Nim (여신님)
- **Angel:** Chun Sa (천사)
- **Honey:** Ja Gee Ya (자기야)
- **Kiss:** Bbo Bbo (뽀뽀)
- **Baby:** Ee Gee Ya (애기야)
- **Pretty:** Ye Bbuh Yo (예뻐요)

> **I love you:** Sa Lang Hee (사랑해)

To add some fun and gamification to the Korean language learning process my wife and I drew up a list of around 50 Korean words/phrases for me to learn initially. To add some extra motivation my wife said that she would give me treat if I could pass a test with 100%. After around 8 weeks of studying I was ready for my first test. I even did a quick revision session to prepare for the test with one of the Korean ladies who was my unofficial tutor. I passed the test with 100% and claimed the treat that my wife had promised me.

Watching a Korean Drama (KDrama) with your lady is a fun activity, but from my personal experience it will be almost impossible to learn Korean from watching Korean dramas. However, as your vocabulary increases you will be able to recognise the odd word or phrase in the show. The same goes for listening to Korean Pop (KPop) music. It's fun and the videos are visually impressive, but again in my experience this will not the best way to learn Korean.

In summary, it is important to learn some basic Korean words to communicate better with your lady and to express your emotions to her. You could try to learn Korean from a formal classroom course, an online course, books or YouTube videos. But don't expect to become fluent in Korean by watching KDrama or listing to KPop.

Alexander James

CHAPTER 9:
KOREAN FOOD AND DRINK

As with every country South Korea has its own local culinary delicacies and local drinks. A Singaporean colleague once shared with me that it would be hard for a Western man to date an Asian lady if he does not enjoy the national cuisine of her home country. When in Asia eat rice not potatoes, was his advice.

Generally, the food in Korea is not as scary or challenging as it can be in Japan or China. However, it can be very hot and spicy similar to the food from Thailand depending on the particular dish ordered. The two most popular and well-known Korean dishes are Bulgogi (불고기) and Bibimbap (비빔밥), which both have high quality meat, typically beef at their centre.

Bulgogi which translates as "fire meat" is a dish of thin, marinated slices of beef grilled on a barbecue. In many restaurants you can have the meat cooked at your table or have it prepared in the kitchen and served to you. In Seoul you can find a version of Bulgogi called Basac (바싹 불고기), which means crispy. In this version the meat is minced rather than sliced and grilled over the barbecue between two fine wire meshes. This is my personal favourite Korean meal.

Bibimbap which translates as "mixed rice" is a dish served in a large china bowl or alternately a hot stone bowl. Vegetables, with chili sauce, a fried egg and thinly sliced grilled beef are served on top of a bed of rice. All of the ingredients are stirred together in the bowl before being eaten.

Kimchi is served as a side dish with almost every meal in Korea. It is made from fermented vegetables, most commonly cabbage and radishes, but there are many varieties. The longer the Kimchi has been fermenting the stronger the taste will be. Most families have a separate Kimchi refrigerator in addition to their normal refrigerator solely for the purpose of making and storing Kimchi. I was amazed at the size and sophistication of these Kimchi refrigerator when my wife showed them to me. They have multiple compartments that can be individually climate controlled for temperature and humidity. For a female celebrity being selected a Kimchi refrigerator model for an advertising campaign is a very prestigious thing in Korea.

One point to note is that many restaurants close at around 9pm which is early by western standards. After this time only the bars are open, where they serve an interesting range of bar snacks. It is important to align the bar snack to the meal. For example, if you are drinking beer then popular bar snacks would be fried chicken, french fries or sun dried squid with peanuts. However, if you are drinking soju then a hot and spicy soup or a kimchi pancake would be a common snack to consume alongside your drink.

Korea also has some interesting street food that you may get to try at some point. Some delicious examples include egg bread (my wife's favourite), spicy rice cakes, tornado potato, fish cakes, deep fried giant squid and Korean soft serve ice cream. The ice crema is severed in a cone at an almost unbelievable height of 32cm. Unless you have very long arms, you will need to get someone else to hold the cone while you eat it.

When it comes to desert you will find cakes, waffles and ice cream which are similar to those that you will find in many other countries. However, the Bingsu is a unique Korean desert that you should try. At first glance it may appear similar to the shaved ice cafes that have become popular in Asia recently. However, it is quite different and much better.

When I tried a shaved ice desert in Hong Kong a couple of years ago, I was very disappointed. After a couple of minutes, the shaved ice became stuck together and you are then left with a giant ice cube. Whereas Bingsu is made from frozen milk, and the shavings remain separate making for a much more enjoyable desert experience. Bingsu is perfect on hot summer days in Korea and comes in many flavours including chocolate, mango, matcha and red bean.

When there is major sporting event like the World Cup or Olympics taking place in South Korea the consumption of dog meat is raised by animal welfare organisations. Yes, it is true that Koreans eat dog meat in the same way that the French eat horse meat. Dog meat is said to have several health benefits including increased energy. However, dog meat is eaten by a very small number of Korean people and it is highly unlikely that you will encounter it during your dating experiences. My wife has only been to a restaurant that serves dog meat once in all of the years that she lived in Korea. As soon as she realised that dog meat was being served, she left the restaurant immediately.

One unique menu item that you may come across in Korea is the couple set meal. Typically, these can be found in fast food style eateries like pizza restaurants and burger restaurants. For example, an Italian restaurant might have a couple set meal with pasta for the lady, pizza for the man, two glasses of soda and a tiramisu dessert to share. Not only does the couple set meal make ordering easier, but the cost is slightly less than ordering the menu items separately.

If you are interested to learn more about food in Korea then I can recommend the "영국남자 Korean Englishman" channel on YouTube. Here you will find lots of interesting and entertaining videos on local Korean dishes.

There are plenty of international restaurants in the major cities and you can find cuisine from almost every country, even North Korea. When planning a date with a Korean lady you should take her to an international restaurant as these perceived as being more special and romantic than Korean restaurants. Italian and Thai are both good options from my experience. You can also try ordering for your Korean lady at restaurants, but only after she has selected her meal (unless of course she asks you to pick a dish for her).

Do not take your Korean lady to restaurants and bars that you would go to with your friends, at least not at the start of your relationship. You should take her somewhere special where she can enjoy being romanced.

In Europe the Russian's have a well-deserved reputation for being heavy drinkers, especially of spirits like Vodka. However, in 2014 a study was published which found that when it comes to spirits that South Koreans drink twice as much as the Russians, and five times as much as the British. The average person in South Korea was drinking almost 14 shots per week. Earlier in my wife's career when she was working in Seoul she was once asked at the end of a job interview how much she could drink. Therefore, I would not recommend challenging any Korean, male or female to a drinking contest as you are likely to come off second best.

In South Korea there are two main types of alcohol that is consumed, beer and the local spirit called Soju.

Soju is a clear spirt that is in some ways similar to Japanese sake or Russian vodka. Soju is only drunk in restaurants and bars, whereas beer is also consumed in the home. Soju is served in small shot glasses and drunk with friends and colleagues. You should never pour your own Soju as this is considered poor etiquette, either because you are drinking alone, or the person who should be pouring the Soju for you is not respecting you by leaving your glass empty. In a business context the junior employees pour for the more senior managers as a mark of respect. However, this is not relevant for a romantic date, unless of course you are dating you manager.

The most important word to learn when drinking with Koreans is:
> **Cheers:** Gun Bay (건배)

Korean beers are generally quite light with a fresh clean taste. Sometimes it can take too long to get drunk by drinking beer alone, so Korean's put Soju in their beer. This is called a "Soju Bomb" and can be very dangerous.

Beer and Soju prices are kept at modest levels so that everyone can afford to have a drink. In Korea drinking is seen as a personal right, similar to people in the US having the right to own and carry a gun. Given the affordable prices and hard drinking culture it is not It is not uncommon to see Korean men drunk or passed out in the street late at night. However, it will be very rare to find a lady in this state, think back to my earlier points about ladies preserving their reputation.

Drinking coffee is very popular in Korea. I regularly travel to the US including Seattle, the home of Starbucks, on business but I was amazed to find that there are even more coffee shops in Seoul than in Seattle. In fact, in 2015 Seoul had 284 Starbucks stores, which is the most of any city in the world, and seven more outlets than New York City in the US.

In addition to the American chains like Starbucks and The Coffee Bean & Tea Leaf, there are multiple local brands including A Twosome Place, Angel-in-us, Paris Baguette, Caffe Bene, dal.komm Coffee, Hollys Coffee, Tom N Toms Coffee, Coffeesmith, Ediya Coffee and Paik's Coffee.

I would also recommend making a note of your ladies' favourite coffee shop and drink so that you can order it for her when on a date. Unfortunately, my wife always changes her coffee order depending on how she is feeling at the time, so this does not work for me.

As you can see Koreans really love their coffee and there is no shortage of places to drink it. However, Korean coffee shops are more than places where people rush in and grab a takeout. They are social meeting places where Koreans gather with friends rather than meeting in their homes which can often be too small to accommodate these groups.

In summary, find some local dishes that you can order and eat when you go to a Korean restaurant, I would recommend Bulgogi and Bibimbap as good options to start with as both are delicious. However, when taking a lady on a date an international restaurant is preferred, Italian and Thai are both good options. Understand that Korea has a big drinking culture and that there is an etiquette to pouring drinks for your companions. Similarly, coffee is very popular, so find out which coffee shops are your dates favourites and arrange to meet up there for a drink.

Alexander James

CHAPTER 10:
IN THE BEDROOM

Korea is a conservative society where women are often not treated with equality to men. Similarly, virginity or at least the perception of virginity is more important for ladies than for men. Therefore, you should protect your Korean ladies' reputation if you are sleeping together. Many Korean men would prefer that their wives are virgins, but that expectation is changing as values and society becomes more progressive.

Like every country you can find Korean girls who are looking for a one-night stand or a "friends with benefits" style of relationship, especially if you go to Itaewon and Hongdae. However, this book is written for the gentleman looking to build a long-term successful relationship with a special Korean lady.

As we discussed in the chapter on Counting the Days, the first 100 day celebration is a big milestone in a couple's relationship. Many Korean ladies will wait until at least 100 days before making love with you for the first time. But every lady is different, some will be happy to be intimate sooner, other will want to wait longer.

My number one recommendation is to go slowly and show respect. Be the gentleman than romances her into bed, show her that you are responsible and caring. And she will let you know when the time is right for her to take the next step in your relationship together.

You will also find that Korean ladies wait longer than western ladies before losing their virginity. The average age in Korea is 22 whereas it is 18 in the UK.

Unlike the UK, Europe and America the oral birth control e.g. The Pill is not common in Korea as Korean ladies are worried about the impact of the hormones on their bodies. In fact, asking a Korean lady to take The Pill will probably end in an argument and no sex. The condom is the preferred method of contraception for most Koreans, and the man is expected to take responsibility. As we know the condom can prevent pregnancy and protect both partners from sexually transmitted diseases. Therefore, if you want to sleep with a Korean lady be a gentleman and take her and your protection seriously. This will demonstrate that you are mature, responsible and committed. Which will likely result in more passionate times together.

Before getting intimate with a Korean lady you should be aware that the majority of Korean men are circumcised between 10–15 years of age. Therefore, if you are uncircumcised this may come as a surprise to some Korean ladies who may only have seen or encountered circumcised penises previously. If you have got to this stage in your relationship and you are uncircumcised then this should not be a major barrier, but you might want to discuss this in advance so as to avoid any surprises the first time that you get naked together.

While we are on the subject of penises a study published in 2012 by Richard Lynn, professor of psychology at Ulster University found that of the 113 countries that he surveyed that South Korean men are in the group with the smallest penises. Now we all know that a lady's pleasure is not related to penis size. However, if you are a non-Asian man, your Korean lady might be happily surprised with what you have in your trousers, even if you are only average by western standards.

While we are talking of size, the average bra size in South Korea is an A cup. However, many Korean ladies wear a bra that is one or more cup sizes larger than fits them to accentuate the curves of their body. Therefore, do not be surprised if when you take off your lady's bra for the first time that her breasts are smaller than you might have anticipated based on her clothed appearance.

Koreans use the word sokgunghap (속궁합) to describe if a couple match in the bedroom or are sexually compatible. As when dating, a Korean lady will also expect the gentlemen to lead in the bedroom, or whichever location you have selected to make love together. She will likely be just as excited and curious to make love with a non-Korean man as you are to make love with a beautiful Korean lady. However, even if she wants you to take her right there and then, she is highly unlikely that she will say so or to initiate intimacy.

She may even resist your advances (to protect her reputation) even if she wants the same thing that you do. Of course, you should make sure that sex is always consensual on both sides and never pressure a lady into making love with you. Rather this is more of a heads up that the Korean lady will probably expect you to take the lead in the bedroom rather than jumping on you and ripping your clothes off.

Korean ladies can be shy, passive and even submissive when it comes to having sex. At least in part this can be attributed to a society that outside of KPop groups is not particularly receptive to ladies expressing their sexuality. For example, the lady may want to keep the lights off in the bedroom to protect her modesty. Additionally, she may be shy to show you her naked body even after making love.

However, many Korean ladies want to enjoy sex and they have a strong desire to make you happy both inside and outside of the bedroom. Therefore, always invest extra time to ensure that she is comfortable and relaxed with you before escalating the passion.

My impression is that many Korean men are selfish lovers and that they only want to have sex for their own enjoyment rather than mutual pleasure for both partners. Or they mistakenly believe that providing expensive gifts is more important than providing sexual pleasure to the lady.

Korean men are generally not particularly affectionate unless they want to have sex. Whereas Westerner men have a reputation for being more romantic, considerate and passionate lovers than Korean men. Therefore, if you focus on the Korean lady's pleasure before your own and show that you care about her enjoyment in the bedroom you have the potential to be her best ever lover.

In Chapter 7: Always on Call we discussed the heavy use of social media and that all ladies are in competition with each other. However, the one thing that a Korean lady is unlikely to share with her friends online or otherwise is details of what happen in the bedroom. You should so the same, never share intimate details and always respect her reputation.

Many Koreans live at home until they get married, therefore you may think that it would be hard for couples to find somewhere private for passionate times together. But this is not the case, as South Korea has many "Love Hotels" designed specifically for couples to enjoy intimate times together. Some feature a fully automated check-in process to avoid the embarrassment of meeting the receptionist who knows why you are there. Some hotels have themed rooms to create more novelty and excitement. In recent years, these establishments have increased their quality and cleanliness significantly to match regular hotels.

It may be a slightly old-fashioned phrase, but some Korean ladies may refer to the highest point of sexual pleasure (aka the Orgasm) as "going to Hong Kong". The historical meaning of this going to Hong Kong relates to when South Korea was still a developing country in the 60s and 70s following World War II. Hong Kong was an aspirational place to visit, more so than China that was less developed and Japan which had previously invaded and occupied the Korean peninsula.

Hong Kong was seen by Koreans as a sophisticated, glamorous and was famous for its nightlife. It was said that anyone who visits Hong Kong would have a very pleasurable time. Over time the term was also used as a euphemism for when achieving the peak of pleasure in the bedroom. Korean ladies are keen to please their partner. Therefore, if you treat your Korean lady with respect, protect her reputation and put her pleasure first you will likely have a very enjoyable and passionate time together.

In summary, it is important to protect the Korean lady's reputation and using a condom is the preferred method of contraception. A Korean lady can be passive and will expect the man to take the lead in the bedroom. There are many Love Hotels in Korea that can provide couples who live together with their parents some private time. Romance your Korean lady into bed and become her personal pilot taking her to Hong Kong as a frequent flyer.

How to Date a Korean Lady

Alexander James

CHAPTER 11:
MEETING HER PARENTS

Family is very important to Koreans, and parents in Korean can have a much larger influence on their children's romantic relationships than would be the case in the UK. This can go as far as a son or daughter ending a relationship simply because they parents do not approve of their choice of partner. Do not underestimate the power of her parents in your relationship.

You should also appreciate that Korean parents are either open to an international partner for their daughter or they are strongly opposed to an international partner daughter.

In the UK your girlfriend would typically come for Sunday dinner or for a BBQ to meet you parents in a casual and relaxed setting. However, this is very different in Korea. A Korean lady or man for that matter would only introduce their partner to their parents when they are ready to get married, which can significantly ramp up the pressure at that first meeting. Therefore, if your Korean lady suggests meeting her parents you should be aware of the significance of this meeting and how her parents will also interpret the intention of this meeting.

Traditionally the lady will meet the man's parents first as the approval of the man parents is most important. If they do not like the lady, then they will not support the marriage, and therefore there is no need for the man to meet the lady's parents. Society is changing, and this will not be the case for all Korean families, however this is how it has been historically. When the times comes how can you make a good impression during the first meeting with her parents?

Firstly, make sure that you are well dressed and well groomed, first impressions are important, and you want her parents to see you as a suitable match for their daughter. Make sure you wear new socks that don't have holes as you will need to remove your shoes when entering her parents' house.

If you are not comfortable sitting on the floor for extended periods of time let your lady know in advance so that she can work with her parents to arrange an alternative. Personally, I have not sat on the floor since primary school. Therefore, sitting on the floor for more than 15-20 minutes becomes increasingly uncomfortable.

Secondly, bring a gift, especially for the lady's mother. One of my female Korean friends explained that her brother took a big bunch of flowers to give to his future Korean mother-in-law at the first meeting. His now mother-in-law was very impressed and still talks about this kind gesture several years later. For the father a nice bottle of alcohol from your home country would be an appropriate gift.

Thirdly, try to use as much Korean as possible when speaking with her parents. It is highly likely that they will not speak any English, so making an effort to speak even a few works of Korean will be very much appreciated. Building up on the phrases we covered in Chapter 8: Learning Korean there are two additional works that it would be good to learn are:

- ➢ **Mother:** Ar Muh Nim (어머님)
- ➢ **Father:** Aa Buh Nim (아버님)

These meanings are not direct translations from Korean into English, and they are probably closer to Aunty and Uncle. That being an older person who is close to you and whom you respect. It would be good to check with your Korean lady to ensure that her parents are agreeable to you using these words to address them. They most likely will be, but it never hurts to ask as you can only make one first impression.

If your future mother-in-law offers you the opportunity to try her home cooking or some of her homemade kimchi accept enthusiastically and share how delicious it is after trying it. Two more good word to learn before meeting her parents are:

- ➢ **Delicious:** Ma Shi Sar Yo (맛있어요)
- ➢ **Tastes Good:** Matt Jo AA Yo (맛좋아요)

Fourthly, be a gentleman, show respect for their daughter in front of her parents. Many parents, especially her father, will not be comfortable with overt displays of affection, so minimise the kissing and hugging during this first meeting. Try to follow Korea etiquette as much as you can, for example bowing to her parents, standing up when a more senior person enters the room and using both hands when you shake hands.

When I met my wife's parents in Korea for the first time, she had explained to them in advance that this not the traditional we are ready to get married meeting as we were an international couple and our relationship was different.

However, within the first 20 minutes of meeting her father outside of the restaurant where I was to be introduced to the whole family. Her father asked me if I was going to marry his daughter that year. Similarly, over desert at the end of the meal her mother asked how many people we were going to invite to our wedding. So even with the advance briefing from my wife the traditional expectations were hard to overcome.

Luckily, I was expecting that the marriage question might come up, so I was prepared to answer this question. I did so by explaining that I was committed to a long-term relationship with their daughter. That we had talked about marriage as a future step, but we were not ready to take that step in this calendar year.

In summary, a Korean lady will only introduce you to their parents when they are ready to get married. Therefore, making a good first impression is very important. Dress smartly, bring gifts, especially flowers for her mother, try to use as much Korean as possible and follow Korean etiquette. And be prepared for the "when are you going to get married?" question if the meeting goes well.

How to Date a Korean Lady

Alexander James

CHAPTER 12: GETTING MARRIED

After the couple have met both sets of parents individually and received their blessing it is time for the couple, and both sets of parents to meet. Again, in the UK both sets of parents would probably meet several times in casual settings before the topic of marriage is raised. Not so in Korea. Marriage in Korea is very much the joining of two families rather than the union of two individuals.

The first time the couple and both sets of parents meet will be at a formal lunch or dinner meeting. This will be in a dedicated dining room away from other guests, and there are even restaurants set up just to cater to these initial parental meetings.

If things go well at this meeting, then the parents will jointly set a date for the wedding. The couple may or may not have a say in the date setting process depending on the family dynamics.

In the UK a couple would typically date for 3-5 years before getting engaged and then be engaged for 1-2 years before actually getting married. However, Korean couples move much faster from first date to marriage. For a Korean lady in her thirties the time from first date to her wedding day could be less than 1 year. The time between the first parents meeting and the wedding ceremony can be as short as 3 months. This can give the impression that it is a shotgun wedding where the bride is pregnant, even to other Koreans. Sometimes this may be the case, but it is not in the majority of instances.

Similarly, in the UK couples frequently live together before getting married as a good way to confirm compatibility. However, it is very rare for Korea couples to live together before marriage. Just 0.2% of Korean households are composed of unmarried couples, whereas this is over 10% in the UK, and almost 20% in Sweden. Think back to the points that we discussed in several chapters about protecting the lady's reputation.

As Korean society does not allow couples to cohabit outside of marriage, this can lead to young couples rushing into marriage before they are ready, just so that they can progress to the next stage of their lives. This is turn is leading to an increased divorce rates in Korea.

Not all grooms propose to their brides in Korea, but if they do then it takes place between the meeting of the parents where the date of the wedding is set, and the actual wedding itself. For those grooms who do decide to propose that it typically follows the western style of presenting the lady with a diamond engagement ring. This can be a small intimate proposal or a large and lavish proposal depending on the individual couple. If the groom does not propose to the bride, then he will probably give a diamond ring to his wife as part of the wedding gifts.

In my case we had set the wedding date and reserved the venue before I proposed, so I was hopefully of a positive response to my proposal which I made at the top of a mountain in Switzerland.

When it is time for you to make a marriage proposal to your Korean lady, I would highly recommend doing this in Korean. I asked one of Korean tutors to teach me how to say this most romantic phase. It was hard to remember and even more difficult to say. But with a couple of weeks of practice I got perfected as follows:

> - **My love, Will you get married with me?** Nae Sarang, JhoWa KyRoonHey JuLayYo? (내사랑, 저와 결혼해 줄래요?)

So, there I was, down on one knee with a sparking diamond ring in my hand and I asked this question to my wife. At first, she was so surprised that I asked her to marry me in Korean that she was speechless. Then she asked me to say it again so that she could hear it property before giving her answer. Luckily, she said yes in Korean, so all my practice of this key phrase paid off at the crucial moment.

As we discussed in Chapter 4: How to Behave on a Date the way in which Korean couples manage money is rather different to couples in the UK, and the wedding costs are no different. Historically, each family in Korea is responsible for a different set of cost in relation to the wedding and setting up life together.

Typically, the groom's family would be responsible for purchasing, or at least putting down a large deposit on an apartment. Whereas the bride's family would be responsible for furnishing the apartment, including all furniture, kitchen appliances, television etc. The cost of the wedding ceremony including venue, photographer, dress, flowers, meal etc. and honeymoon is typically divided equally between both families. In addition, each family will buy gifts for the other family.

In the past the parents of Korean couples have picked up the majority of the costs for their children's weddings and a home for the married couple. However, today given the increased costs of buying an apartment, families are sharing these costs rather than the burden falling only on the husband's family. The couple may also contribute a greater proportion than has been the case in the past. In our case my wife and I covered all of our wedding costs and did not ask either of our parents to contribute financially.

Not all newly married couples can afford to buy an apartment when they get married, even with the support of their families. Therefore, the couple may rent rather than buying. Similarly, it is not uncommon for the couple to live with the husband's parents initially while they save up for their own apartment. This would be practically unheard of in the UK. Living with her in-laws can also put a lot of pressure and obligation on a Korean lady, so she will be keen to avoid this situation if at all possible.

In the UK weddings can take place at a church or any venue that has been officially certified for the purpose of holding marriage ceremonies. Some people get married at their university, or a stately home or even on the beach. Others choose to get married inside the stadium of their favourite sports team, for example the Old Trafford stadium is a popular venue for committed Manchester United fans.

In Korea most wedding ceremonies take place in wedding hall designed specifically for the purpose. Rather like a multi-screen cinema several weddings can take place at the same time in different rooms within the wedding hall. After the ceremony, the guests will have a buffet style lunch, in some cases the guests from multiple wedding will mingle together at one common buffet.

For couples with larger budgets the wedding ceremony will probably take place at a luxury hotel rather than at a wedding hall. For example, my wife and I got married at a luxury resort hotel overlooking ocean in Busan.

You should also understand that in Korea the wedding ceremony is purely ceremonial, it is a celebration that carries no legal standing. It is only when the couple register their marriage at the local council office that it becomes legal.

Increasing numbers of Korean couples are having a wedding that combines the western style wedding and traditional Korean style wedding ceremonies.

For the Korean style wedding ceremonies both the bride and groom will wear a traditional Korean hanbok. For the lady this combines a large skirt with a high waist band just below the bust. Over the top of this the lady wears a short jacket with long sleeves. For the man there is a pair of trousers with long jacket, again with long sleeves. On my wedding day several of my friends described me as looking like a Jedi knight from Star Wars in my hanbok.

The traditional Korean wedding ceremony is called the Pyebaek and takes place in a special room. Typically, only direct family are invited to participate in the Pyebaek ceremony. However, as my wife and I had a small wedding with only 20 guests, some who had travelled from UK, Hong Kong, Malaysia and America to join us in Busan, we invited everyone to join the Pyebaek ceremony and to share in the experience.

Initially the man's parents will be seated on the floor at the front of the room behind a low table with dried fruits and a pair of wedding ducks. The couple will bow to his parents to show respect and then serve them a drink, assisted by a helper as it is difficult to move around easily when wearing hanboks.

The man's parents will provide some words of wisdom to the couple for their married life together. They will then present the couple with an envelope containing money that couple can use for their life together.

The couple then turn to face each other, and the groom holds the end of the bride's apron, forming a kind of hammock. His parents then throw Dates and Chestnuts for the couple to catch in the brides outstretched apron. The number of Dates caught signifies the number of boys and Chestnuts caught the number of girls that the couple will have.

This process is then repeated for the bride's parents. This process can also be repeated for other serious members of both families, but on our wedding day we limited it to just our parents.

The couple then move to the front of the room and serve each other a drink which they then consume with linked arms. The Pyebaek ceremony concludes with the groom giving the bride a piggyback ride around the room. This is to demonstrate to everyone that he is capable (quite literally) of supporting his wife in their future life together. So, make sure that you are maxing out your squats in the gym prior to the wedding day.

I was nervous about potentially dropping my wife, not because she was heavy, rather because the multiple layers of fabric made it very hard to grip her securely. However, the piggyback ride around the room was completed without incident. Sometimes the groom will also give his mother-in-law a piggyback ride as well, luckily for me my mother-in-law politely declined this tradition.

In summary, Korean couples move quickly from dating to marriage and their parents' input is more important than in the UK. The wedding costs and the costs of setting up home together are typically split between the two families. The wedding day frequently combines both western and Korean style ceremonies, with the Korean ceremony concluding with the groom giving his bride a piggyback ride around the room.

Alexander James

SUMMARY

In summary if you try to date a Korean lady as you would date a western lady you will probably fail. You need to date a Korean lady as a Korean man would date her to be successful and win her heart.

In Chapter 1 we explored why Korean ladies are the most desirable in Asia, why they have high expectations for any man who wants to date them, and reviewed the importance of being a successful man and presenting yourself well.

In Chapter 2 we discussed how to make the initial connection with a Korean lady via mutual friends, the use of online and mobile dating apps and the importance of being clear in explaining your intentions. If you don't tell the Korean lady that you want to be more than friends, she will not know.

In Chapter 3 we looked at the importance of leading the date course and how this can help the lady to reconnect with her feminine side. We explored how being organised can help the man to minimise any potential stress from the expectation to lead.

In Chapter 4 we examined how to be a gentleman on a date, some of the prejudices that you many encounter as an international couple, who pays the bill on a date and how Korean couples manage their money after marriage.

In Chapter 5 we explored couple style and why Korean couples like to dress alike to show that they are in a relationship in a more reserved society that is less open to physical displays of affection.

In Chapter 6 we discussed the importance of counting the days in Korean relationships, the many special days on which couples in Korea may choose to celebrate their relationship, and the complexity of celebrating birthdays based on the Lunar calendar.

In Chapter 7 we explored the use of mobile messaging using KakaoTalk and the importance of responding to messages promptly, always being ready to take a photo or appear in a photo, and the availability of couple apps.

In Chapter 8 we identified that it is important to lean some basic Korean words to communicate better with your Korean lady and to express your emotions to her. Techniques that you could try to learn Korean include formal classroom courses, online course, books and YouTube videos.

In Chapter 9 we explored some local Korean dishes and confirmed that international restaurants are better options for a date. We identified that Korea has a big drinking culture, explained the etiquette of pouring Soju, and confirmed that Coffee is very popular in Korea.

In Chapter 10 we identified the importance of protect the Korean lady's reputation, that as with dating a Korean lady will expect the gentleman to take the lead in the bedroom, and that you should be her personal pilot and make her a frequent flyer to Hong Kong.

In Chapter 11 we identified the importance of being introduced to your partner's parents, reviewed guidance for making a good first impression, and the need to be prepared for the "when are you going to get married?" question.

In Chapter 12 we looked at the first meeting between the two sets of parents, making your proposal in Korean and the wedding day including the traditional Korean Pyebaek ceremony and the significance of the piggyback ride.

I would like to conclude by repeating that the advice in this book is based on my personal experience of dating and marrying one Korean lady, inputs from other Korean ladies in international relationships and reading online articles. Every lady is unique and special so not every piece of advice in this book will be applicable to every Korean lady.

However, by having a greater understanding and awareness of the unique elements of dating in Korea you should be more prepared to build a successful long-term relationship with a Korean lady.

Always remember that if you try to date a Korean lady as you would date a western lady, you will fail. You need to learn to date her as a Korean man would date her if you want to be successful.

Finally, if you've found this book useful, please consider leaving a short review on Amazon.

Made in the USA
Middletown, DE
12 November 2022